HOW TO SETUP APPLE WATCH

The Complete Beginner to Pro Setup Guide

By

ROLAND SUMMER
Copyright©2018

COPYRIGHT

TABLE OF CONTENT

CHAPTER ONE
INTRODUCTION

The Apple watch is our favorite gadgets and represents a new way people relate to technology. This device enables you to communicate in various ways, like pictures of your fitness and health, play music, Install apps, time, messages on the go and many more.

The Apple watch and iphone may be two different pieces of hardware, but one can't work without the other. Once you get a brand new Apple watch, turning it on is the first step, next comes paring it with an iphone. When it comes time to pair your Apple watch with your iphone (or via App store, if you have deleted it previously).

CHAPTER TWO

CHARGE YOUR GADGET

Your watch most comes with some battery life, it's generally advice to fully charge any pieces of electronics when you first use it. Plug in your watch and leave it while you set it up for the first time if the watch doesn't power on as you plug in your charger press the side button (not the digital crown) to turn it on.

PAIR THE WATCH WITH YOUR IPHONE

Your watch will show you a screen asking you to choose a language. Choose one that you will understand perfectly, and then wait for a while for the watch to configure itself, you will see a pop-up on the screen asking you to open the Apple watch app on your iphone, which Apple has helpfully pre-installed with the last iphone update. Do it and hit the prompt on the apple watch.

The watch will pop-up a blue bubble of undulating dots, while the iphone will open the camera and instruct you to center the viewfinder on the watch. This process is quite simple as scanning a QR code.

If the camera-based paring isn't working for any reason, you can tap the "I" button on the watch to give a six digit code, which you can enter on your iphone to pair the two device together.

Roland Summer

CHAPTER THREE

SELECT YOUR WRIST PREFERENCE AND PRESS A BUNCH OF BUTTONS

You will need to choose a wrist preference, right or left Apple watch works on either. Once you are done that you'll need to accept the terms of service. Also register your apple watch with Apple via your Apple ID during this process; you will see series of setup notice for location service and diagnostic the watch will pull the settings for each of these from your iphone. Turn on your location for your iphone, it will be available to the watch.

SET UP SECURITY AND CHOOSE YOUR WATCH APPS

Your Apple watch will ask you to set up a numeric pass code on your watch with your phone, accept it simply implies that as long as your watch stays on your wrist it remains unlock. If you take it off it will request the pass code to use it again. When its on your wrist, unlocking your phone will also unlock the watch.

The option you'll see offers to pre-install apps on your Watch as a comprehensive batch, instead of making you do it one by one. This is your choice, but having a bunch of apps on the Watch doesn't seem to harm anything, so you may as well let it install them all.

Apps are just little extensions of the apps that are already installed on your phone, so there's a very good chance you have a bunch of them already! You will manage what is and isn't installed on your watch in a later step via the iPhone's Watch app.

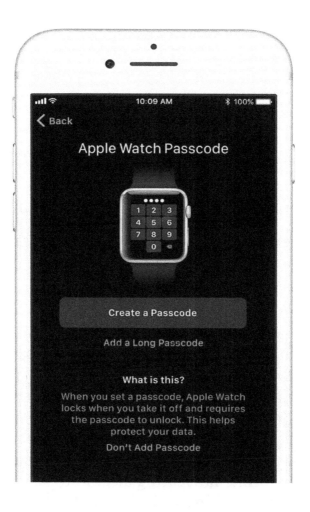

DRIVE INTO YOUR SETTINGS

We'll educate you on how to setup features, like SOS and Activity. On Apple Watch Series 3 (GPS + Cellular).

Then you can install your apps that are compatible with Apple Watch.

Just like your iphone Apple watch has a huge array of settings to go through. You can adjust some of them on the app settings, its faster and easier to do most of this on your iphone- the settings sync over quickly. The settings are split into few sections, with general package at the top and app-by-app settings underneath. There are a ton of settings, try to spend some time navigating around to see if there is anything you will love to change, but for most of this you can go on with the defaults.

We advise you to look at the sounds and haptics. That's where you set how loud your watch beeps when notifications pops

(suggestion: don't let it beep at all). You can also enable the strength of the haptics which is how hard the watch taps you when get alert. Some find the max setting is the best. And if you still and if you can't still feel it, you can turn on prominent Haptics, which does Exactly what it says: it makes your watch really vibrate a lot before the regular tap when you get a notification.

APPLE PAY SETUP

You can use apple pay on your watch by clicking on the main button, but its not set up with your card out of the box. To set it up, head on down to the app settings for passbook and Apple Pay on your phone's Apple Watch app.
Here you'll find many places where you have the option to "mirror my phone ," which means the cards you see on the phone also show up on your watch. That don't apply to credit cards, though you will need to click "Add Credit or Debit Card" to get one activated and approved from your watch.
When you wish to pay, Double click that button. The watch can only grant you pay after it's been attached to your wrist and have unlocked your iphone with TouchD, random people won't be able to pay for stuff with your watch.(The watch don't know whose wrist it's

on though; someone can equally put it on and you unlock your phone, they'll be able to pay with your card.

CHAPTER FOUR

SET UP ACTIVITY APP

Apple has few system built into the Apple watch for tracking your health. There's and a heart rate monitor for exercise but the one that you'll definitely love the most is the activity app. It can track your steps and general activity level three daily meters: movement, exercise and time spent standing. It can annoy you to stand up from time to time which is helpful But it can't perform such activity until you've set up the app. Some have reasons for not turning it on, but most it's a nice little way to make sure you're not being too lazy.
To set it up, open the app up (horray, your first watch app) on the watch to get it done click the digital crown until you're looking at the app grid an array of circular icons set out in a honeycomb pattern. Stick around until you see the activity app; it looks like three concentric circles. Once you are done you'll

also have the active app show up on your iphone.

Click on all the details on the watch screen.
Finally if you wish you can enter your body info into the health section of the preferences app, if there's something you want to track.

CUSTOMIZE YOUR NOTIFICATIONS

Go back to the Apple watch app on your iphone and drill into notifications. By default, everything that all that notifies you on your iphone will also notify you on your watch. You have not done much clean up of what gets to notify you on your phone. "That your Turn" notification from words with friends might not be that friendly on your phone, but on your watch it is very annoying.
Please go through that section of the watch app turn off anything you don't want to see on your wrist. It'll be on your phone Apple Apps that have watch-specific settings are at the top, mirroring options underneath. You can also choose a red dot as a missed notifications indicator.

SET UP SOME MUSIC AND BLUETOOTH HEADPHONES

Your Apple Watch can work without your iPhone right there with you, including playing music for your workout. But to do it, you'll have to click into iTunes or the Music app on your phone to select some music over to the Watch. You can equally Set up a playlist, then find the settings for Music in the Watch app on your iPhone, and that's where you pick your playlist. You most have to do this now because it takes a little while for the music to sync, and it needs to be sitting on the charger for it to happen.

Apple Watch don't have a headphone jack, so you'll need a setup a Bluetooth headphones to listen to music without your iPhone present.

CHOOSE AND ORGANIZE YOUR GLANCE

Glances, you can recall, the small info screens you access by swiping up from the watch face. There are a lot of them, and having to swipe through stuff you absolutely don't care about to access stuff that you do care about is annoying. The perfect way to do that is from the Glances setting in the app. It works the same way as the organization page for Notification Center. You can rearrange glances or hit the minus button to take them off your watch.

You can also toggle Glances inside each app's main settings page. you can move down on the main screen of the Watch app, where all the installed apps are listed. If you click on each one, you'll find another notification option here and also, with many of them, the option to toggle a "Glance."

CHAPTER FIVE

ORGANIZE YOUR APPS AND SET PREFERENCES

All apps on your Apple Watch are organized in a honeycomb pattern. The Watch is the app itself, and it will always be at the center. You can roll the Digital Crown to zoom in to sections of your choice, or pan around to tap the one you want. There are some apps you use frequently you might as well place them near the center. To get it done, go into the App Layout of the Watch app on your iPhone and move them around with a long-press.

You can also move back to the main screen and poke around the individual settings for the main Apple apps. One app that would be good to weak: Mail. That's where you decide which mail alerts will come to your wrist. Almost done!

SET UP YOUR CONTACTS

The sequence step! By now, your contacts most be synced over to the phone. You can access your favorites by pressing the button on the side of the Watch, then use the digital crown to scroll through them. Automatically the Watch puts the people you've already marked as favorites here. But if you'd like a different set of folks on your Watch, you can change that in the iPhone's Watch app.

GET UP OFFA THAT THING

That's it! There still might be some data syncing over to the Apple Watch, so don't panic if it feels a little laggy at first. It get better once the sync is complete, but as we outlined in our review, it will always have some load times for apps and glances.

There's still more you COULD do, if you wish. Apple has a very big section for Watch apps if you want to poke around in its store. You can find Apple's favorites in the Featured tab of the Watch App on your iPhone — and here are our favorite Watch apps.

But honestly, you've been sitting for a while, and at some point the Apple Watch is going to tell you that it would be a good idea to stand up. You may as well; that Activity Meter isn't going to fill itself. Congrats on your new watch!

THE END.